Criminal Profiling:

An Introductory Guide

David A. Webb

To Louise, Luca and Paolo with much love.

CONTENTS

A WORD FROM THE AUTHOR 5

ORIGINS OF CRIMINAL PROFILING 8

THE FBI LEGACY 12

BEYOND THE MODUS OPERANDI 24

PUTTING THEORY INTO PRACTICE 27

DOES CRIMINAL PROFILING WORK? 30

GEOGRAPHIC PROFILING 33

BECOMING A PROFILER 37

ACCESS FBI PROFILING PUBLICATIONS 45

A FINAL WORD 46

A WORD FROM THE AUTHOR

Hello and a very warm welcome. My name is David Webb and I've had a passionate interest in psychology for over 20 years. I began studying psychology in 1990, and I've been teaching psychology in some capacity or another since 1998. As a University lecturer I had the opportunity to write and deliver an undergraduate course in forensic psychology, part of which examined criminal profiling.

In recent years criminal profiling has been the subject of a whole host of books, films and television series. However; despite its continued coverage and popular profile very few people get to study the topic in any depth. A main reason for putting this guide together, therefore, was to the make the study of criminal profiling much more accessible. I also hope that this guide will offer a balanced account of criminal profiling, as opposed to the often distorted, sensationalized and inaccurate view promoted in the popular media.

I sincerely hope you find this introductory guide to criminal profiling informative and engaging.

Connect & Learn

Before you begin reading please take a moment to join me and thousands of psychology students online.

Psychology on Facebook

www.facebook.com/psychologyonline

Psychology on Twitter

http://twitter.com/psych101

Psychology on Google+

http://bit.ly/PsychologyGooglePlus

Psychology on Linkedin

www.linkedin.com/groups?about&gid=4016322

Psychology on YouTube

www.youtube.com/user/LearnAboutPsychology

Psychology on Pinterest

http://pinterest.com/psychology/

And please feel free to take a look at the four websites built around my teaching and research interests.

www.all-about-psychology.com

www.all-about-forensic-psychology.com

www.all-about-forensic-science.com

www.all-about-body-language.com

Kind regards.

David Webb BSc (hons), MSc

ORIGINS OF CRIMINAL PROFILING

In order to think about and evaluate criminal profiling from a contemporary perspective you have to have some idea of the way in which it has evolved over the years. With this in mind, we will start by taking a close look at the first widely documented use of profiling within a criminal investigation. The importance of this landmark case cannot be underestimated, as it paved the way for the FBI's highly influential work on criminal profiling. Work which has come to dominate our modern-day understanding of the topic.

Profiling The Mad Bomber

The psychiatrist Dr James A. Brussel is widely credited with undertaking the first systematic offender profile within a criminal investigation. It was the profile of the person responsible for a series of indiscriminate bombing attacks spanning 16 years in New York.

Background To The Case

The first bomb was left at the business premises of the energy utility Consolidated Edison in November 1940. The pipe bomb did not detonate (arguably by design) as when it was discovered it was found to be wrapped in a note stating 'CON EDISON CROOKS, THIS IS FOR YOU'.

A year later a very similar device was discovered. The bomb investigation team concluded that it had been constructed by the same person. The location of the device indicated that the bomber was probably en route to the Consolidated Edison building once again but for some reason he had to abandon his plan and the device was just left on the street.

Up to this point neither incident had been reported in the press.

Three months later as US involvement in the Second World War began the bomber sent a type set letter to the police - it read. 'I will make no more bomb units for the duration of the war - my patriotic feelings have made me decide this - later I will bring the Con Edison to justice - they will pay for their dastardly deeds.' In fact the perpetrator didn't make another bomb for nine years.

It was March 1950 when a third unexploded bomb was discovered and it was felt that it was never intended to go off. However, this was the calm before the storm, a fourth bomb exploded at the New York Public Library followed by another shortly afterwards at Grand Central station. In the next six years over 30 bombs would be planted, the vast majority of which detonated.

Despite the remarkable fact that no one had been killed there was a genuine sense of fear that it was merely a matter of time. Public and political pressure on the police force to apprehend the bomber intensified the longer he remained at large. As a result of this pressure Dr James A. Brussel was asked to generate a profile of the bomber in the hope that it would help focus the investigation.

The Criminal Profile

Male, former employee of Consolidated Edison, injured while working there so seeking revenge, paranoid, 50 years old, neat and meticulous persona, foreign background, some formal education, unmarried, living with female relatives but not mother who probably died when he was young, upon capture he will be wearing a buttoned up double breasted jacket.

The Logic Behind The Profile

Most of the observations were based on common sense e.g. male (like the vast majority of bombers). The profile data relating to his former employer Consolidated Edison were obvious from the content of the letters he posted. Other aspects of the profile were Sherlock Holmes like, take for example the claim that the bomber was foreign. Brussel theorized that this was because the suspect wrote in an over formal way e.g. 'dastardly deeds' and he never used contemporary slang.

In terms of a lasting legacy, however, the most significant parts of the profile were based on Brussel's psychiatric and psychoanalytical interpretations. Brussel believed that the bomber had an 'Oedipus complex' and most Oedipal sufferers tend to be unmarried and live with female relatives, hence it's inclusion in the criminal profile. He formulated this observation on what he saw as the phallic construction of the bombs and the way in which the bomber wrote 'breast-like' W's in the hand written letters he posted. Also when the perpetrator planted bombs in movie theatres, Brussel noted that he would often 'slash' and 'penetrate' the seats.

If you would like to learn more about the Oedipus Complex - see following link to read a classic article on the subject By André Tridon.

www.all-about-psychology.com/oedipus-complex.html

Criminal Profiling Recommendations

Brussel suggested that the police publicize their investigation along with the profile description of the bomber. In Brussel's opinion the bomber wanted credit for his work and this arrogance was likely to be his downfall as he may well be tempted to reveal details that would lead the police to his door.

Every major newspaper in New York gave details of the profile and although this resulted in a number of false leads the real bomber phoned Brussel warning him against any further involvement.

At the same time administrative staff at Consolidated Edison had been instructed to search their employee files for anyone who appeared to match the bombers profile. A member of staff came across the file of George Metesky. Metesky had an accident at work and had filed an unsuccessful disability claim against the company. In response to the failed disability claim Metsky wrote a series of letters to the company, one of which referred to their 'dastardly deeds'.

George Metesky was arrested shortly afterwards and immediately confessed. As he was being escorted to the police station it didn't go unnoticed that he was wearing a buttoned up double breasted jacket!

Having pioneered the use of criminal profiling over a number of years Dr James A. Brussel formally documented his work in 1968 in his book 'casebook of a criminal psychiatrist'.

THE FBI LEGACY

Dr James Brussel's book was read with great interest by Howard Teten a FBI agent who was teaching a course in criminology at the time.

The following extract is taken from an interview Teten gave and it provides a fascinating insight into the FBI's criminal profiling history and approach.

"I developed the FBI's original approach to profiling as a lecture course in 1970. The title of the course was Applied Criminology although several instructors later started calling it Psych-crim. This course was based on a concept which I had originally developed while working as a police crime scene specialist. The idea was conceived in about 1961-62. However, it was necessary to test the approach using solved cases for about 7 years and to check with several Psychiatrists to ensure I was on firm ground in terms of the characteristics of the different mental problem areas before I felt it was ready for presentation...I expanded the course by asking that unsolved cases be brought in for use as examples.

During the class, a profile of the offender was developed for one of the cases being utilized and the perpetrator was identified...our new expanded FBI Academy opened in 1972...new units were also formed to provide the needed oversight and organization necessary to ensure all students received the same material and instruction. One of the units formed was the Behavioral Science Unit.

In 1973, after reading Dr. James Brussel's. "Case Book of a Crime Psychiatrist," I visited Dr. Brussel at his home in New York. While he was for all intents and purposes, retired at that time, he was most gracious and was quite willing to discuss his approach to profiling. Over the next year or so I visited him on several occasions examining the similarities and differences in our approaches. His approach was to seek specific areas of psychiatric potential and then to combine them to form a profile. This was somewhat different from my approach which was to derive an overall impression of the gross mental status based on the crime scene as a whole. We reasoned that his method was more capable of providing detailed information while my approach was less subject to error...

Robert Ressler began conducting interviews with convicted serial killers in 1976. After a number of interviews, he was joined in this project by John Douglas who had joined the BSU in early 1976. This project was able to provide a significant amount of information in terms of why and how certain characteristics were found at the crime scenes." The data from these interviews were particularly valuable in that the information allowed even those profilers who had not conducted a large number of crime scene analyses to be effective in **evaluating the psychological impressions at a crime scene.**"

By the 1980s, the concept of criminal profiling was maturing into a full-fledged investigative tool for identifying criminals and their future actions by studying their behaviors, personalities, and physical traits. In July 1984 the National Center for the Analysis of Violent Crime (NCAVC) was opened for business on the campus of the FBI Academy, Quantico,

13

Virginia.to provide criminal profiling services to state and local police for the first time.

The NCAVC also conducted research into violent crime from a law enforcement perspective designed to gain insight into criminal thought processes, motivations and behavior. Part of this initiative involved disseminating information about criminal profiling and its investigative potential out in the field. For example, the following article by legendary criminal profiler John Douglas and Alan Burgess was first published by the FBI in 1986. At the time, special agent Douglas was *Profiling and Consultation Program Manager* at the NCAVC and Burgess was *Chief of the Behavioral Science Investigative Support Unit* at the NCAVC.

A Viable Investigative Tool Against Violent Crime

Quickly apprehending a perpetrator of a violent crime, rape, homicide, child abduction is a major goal of all law enforcement agencies. Unlike other disciplines concerned with human violence, law enforcement does not, as a primary objective, seek to explain the actions of a violent offender. Instead, its task is to ascertain the identity of the offender based on what is known of his actions. Described by one author as an emitter of signals during commission of a crime,' the criminal must be identified as quickly as possible to prevent further violence. While studies explaining why certain individuals commit violent crimes may aid them in their search, law enforcement investigators must adapt the study findings to suit their own particular needs. Criminal profiling is a tool law enforcement 'may use to combine the results of studies in other disciplines with more traditional techniques in an effort to combat violent crime.

14

The profiling process is defined by the FBI as an investigative technique by which to identify the major personality and behavioral characteristics of the offender based upon an analysis of the Crime(s) he or she has committed. The process generally involves seven steps.

1. Evaluation of the criminal act itself.

2. Comprehensive evaluation of the specifics of the crime scene(s).

3. Comprehensive analysis of the victim.

4. Evaluation of preliminary police reports.

5. Evaluation of the medical examiner's autopsy protocol.

6. Development of profile with critical offender characteristics.

7. Investigative suggestions predicated on construction of the profile.

The process used by the person preparing a criminal personality profile is quite similar to that used by clinicians to make a diagnosis and treatment plan: Data is collected and assessed, the situation reconstructed, hypotheses are formulated, a profile developed and tested, and the results reported back. Criminal personality profiling has been used by law enforcement with success in many areas and is viewed as a way in which the investigating officer can narrow the scope of an investigation. Profiling unfortunately does not provide the identity of the offender, but it does indicate the type of person most likely to have committed a crime having certain unique characteristics.

Profile Applications

One area in which criminal profiling (personality assessment) has been useful is in hostage negotiation. Law enforcement officers need to learn as much as possible about the hostage taker in order to protect the lives of the hostages. They must be able to assess the subject in terms of his probable course of action and his reactions to various stimuli. In such cases, police obtain information about the offender through verbal contact with the hostage taker and possibly through access to his family and associates. Criminal profiling techniques have also been used in identifying anonymous letter writers and persons who make written or spoken threats of violence. In cases of the latter, psycholinguistic techniques have been used to compose a "threat dictionary," whereby every word in a message is assigned, by computer, to a specific category. Words as they are used in the message are then compared to those words as they are used in ordinary speech or writings, and the vocabulary usage of a particular author or speaker may yield "signature" words unique to that individual. In this way, police may not only be able to determine that several letters were written by the same individual but also learn about the background and psychology of the offender.

Rapists and arsonists also lend themselves to criminal profiling techniques. Through careful interview of the rape victim about the rapist's behavior, law enforcement personnel may be able to build a profile of the offender? The theory behind this approach is that behavior (sexual, physical, verbal) reflects personality, and by examining the behavior of the rapist during the assault, the investigator may be able to determine what type of person is responsible for the offense. Common characteristics of arsonists have been derived from an analysis of the Uniform Crime reports. Knowledge of the arsonist's psychodynamics can aid the investigator in identifying possible suspects, predicting location of subsequent arsons, and developing techniques and strategies for interviewing suspects.

Criminal profiling has been useful in investigating sexual homicides because many of these crimes appear motiveless and thus offer few obvious clues about the killer's identity. In murders that result from jealousy or a family quarrel, or take place during commission of a felony, the readily identifiable motive generally provides vital information about the identity of the killer. Because many sexual homicides fail to provide this information, investigators must look to methods that supplement conventional investigative techniques to identify the perpetrator.

Case in Point

Criminal profiling uses the behavioral characteristics of the offender as its basis. Sexual homicides, for example, yield much information about the mind and motivation of the killer. A new dimension is provided to the investigator via the profiling technique, particularly in cases where the underlying motivation for the crime may be suddenly hidden from even the more experienced detective. The following case will illustrate this point.

17

During the fall of 1982, an urban Midwest police department detective telephonically contacted the FBI's Behavioral Science Unit at the FBI Academy asking for some assistance. The detective described in detail the rape/murder of a 25-year-old white married woman. The detective advised that the apartment where the victim was killed had been ransacked, but they were unable to determine at that time if anything was taken by the killer. In view of the fact that many leads were still outstanding and information concerning the autopsy, laboratory examinations, background of the victim, previously reported neighborhood crimes, etc., was still pending, the detective was advised that a profile could not be provided at that time. After approximately 1 week, the detective forwarded the necessary information to the local FBI field office criminal profile coordinator. After reviewing the case for completeness, the profile coordinator forwarded the materials to the Behavioral Science Investigative Support Unit at the FBI Academy for analysis. Color 8 x 10 crime scene photographs re-created the crime and revealed that the victim was killed in her living room, with no evidence of any struggle or defense attempts by her. The victim was lying face up on the living room floor. Her dress was raised up over her hips exposing her genital area, and her panties were pulled down to her knees. The murder weapon (hammer) belonging to the victim was found in kitchen sink, and it appeared that the victim's blood had been washed off the hammer by the subject. Crime scene photographs further revealed that the subject opened dresser drawers and closet doors. Investigative reports indicated the victim's husband advised that jewelry belonging to victim was missing.

The victim and her husband had lived in the apartment for approximately 6 months, and neighbors and associates reported they were friendly and quiet and kept to themselves.

The medical examiner concluded in his protocol that there was no apparent indication that the victim was sexually assaulted. Laboratory reports indicated that the victim had been drinking at the time of the assault, and there was no evidence of semen present in or on the victim or her clothing. From the above information, the criminal profiler advised the detective that he had already interviewed the killer. The surprised detective was presented with the following probable crime scenario.

The victim was drinking with the offender prior to her death. An argument ensued, reaching a threshold where the offender could not take it any longer. Angered, he obtained a "weapon of opportunity" from a kitchen cabinet and returned to the living room where he confronted the victim face to face and repeatedly struck victim about her head and face. After killing her, the offender realized that the police would surely implicate him as the obvious murderer. He then washed blood from his hands in the kitchen sink and also cleaned blood and fingerprints from the hammer. He rolled the victim over in a face-up position and "staged" the crime to appear the way he felt a sexually motivated crime should look. He conducted the staging by making it appear that the offender searched for money or personal property in the apartment.

Upon hearing this analysis of the crime, the detective exclaimed, "You just told me the husband did it.'" the detective was coached regarding suggested re-interview techniques of the victim's husband. In addition, the detective was further advised that if the victim's husband were given a polygraph examination, he in all probability would react more strongly to the known fact that he was "soiled" by his wife's blood than to questions concerning his wife's murder. The detective was told to have the polygraph examiner direct questions at the husband, acknowledging the fact that he got blood on his hands and washed them off along with the hammer in the kitchen sink. About 5 days later, the detective called the criminal profiler to advise that the victim's husband was charged with murder. According to the detective, the husband failed the polygraph and subsequently admitted his guilt to the polygraph examiner.

The Profiling and consultation Program

The FBI's profiling program has grown considerably since the late 1970's from "informal" analysis and profiling during criminal psychology classes at the FBI Academy to the present formalized program. Currently, the program consists of one program manager and seven criminal profilers and crime analysts. These Agents were selected primarily for their investigative experience, expertise, and educational backgrounds. The Behavioral Science Investigative Support Unit has found that anyone seeking transfer into this highly specialized program must possess above all other attributes and accomplishments a strong investigative background that includes participating in, supervising, and managing major case assignments.

During 1985, the Criminal Profiling and Consultation Program received over 600 requests for profiling assistance. It is anticipated that once the FBI's Violent Criminal Apprehension Program (VICAP) is fully operational, the number of profiling requests will nearly double annually. One key link to the success of the FBI's Criminal Profiling Program is its criminal profile coordinators who are located at every one of the FBI's 59 field offices. These highly trained and selected Agents are responsible for screening cases and for providing preliminary investigative suggestions to investigators. While the field coordinators do not have the authority to provide profiles to requesting law enforcement agencies, they are authorized to prepare preliminary "rough draft" profiles which are reviewed by the profiling staff at the FBI Academy prior to being disseminated to the requesting agency.

Criminal profiling is available to local, State, Federal, and foreign law enforcement agencies or departments. It should be noted that not every violent crime matter lends itself to the profiling process. The criminal profile coordinators in the FBI field offices determine during review of the case whether it can be profiled. However, while a case may not be suitable for profiling, the coordinator may still submit it to the Behavioral Science Unit for other types of services. Criminal profilers at the FBI Academy may assist the law enforcement community by providing inter-view/interrogation techniques, investigative suggestions and techniques, establish probable cause for search warrants as a result of National Center for the Analysis of Violent Crime violent offender research findings, assist prosecutors relative to prosecutive strategies, and possibly provide testimony as a witness for the prosecution or as an expert witness during the sentence phase of the trial. All cases must be submitted to the local FBI field office for review and administrative handling by that criminal profile coordinator.

Lt. Commdr. Vernon J. Geberth of the New York City Police Department wrote in his book, Practical Homicide Investigation: Tactics, Procedures and Forensic Techniques, "This program has proven to be beneficial to law enforcement and has provided homicide detectives with a viable investigative tool."

Criminal profiling will never take the place of a thorough and well-planned investigation nor will it ever eliminate the seasoned, highly trained, and skilled detective. Criminal profiling has, however, developed itself to a level where the detective has another investigative weapon available to him in solving a violent crime. The offender, on the other hand, has an added worry that in time he will be identified, indicted, successfully prosecuted, and sentenced for his crime.

(John Douglas & Alan Burgess, 1986)

In essence then, the essential purpose of criminal profiling is to generate a behavioral composite of an unknown offender so that it tells you something about the personality of the individual. How you develop this composite can differ but the end result is the same i.e. establishing an informed sense of the type of person who has committed the crime. A point emphasized in all the following descriptions of criminal profiling.

"An educated attempt to provide specific information about a certain type of suspect." (Geberth, 1981).

"A biographical sketch of behavioral patterns, trends and tendencies.' (Vorpagel, 1982).

"This role (criminal profiling) was obviously not to provide the name, address and phone number of the guilty person but was to provide the police with a psychological profile of the personality of the perpetrator that could then be used to direct the investigative search." (Jackson & Bekerian 1997).

"Profilers have been able to develop typologies, understand the link between crime scenes and the characteristics of offenders, and develop information that is useful in violent crime investigations." (Hinman 2002).

BEYOND THE MODUS OPERANDI

Having established the notion that criminal profiling is employed to uncover the behavioral make-up of an unknown offender, we now turn our attention to the psychological mechanism which proponents of criminal profiling say makes this possible i.e., **signature behavior**.

I'm sure you will have watched a film or TV series where a detective at a crime scene asks 'what's the MO?'. MO stands for Modus Operandi and it literally means way of working, and it's what an offender does in order to carry out a crime. For example, a burglar who always uses a glass cutter to gain access to a house is demonstrating an aspect of his or her MO or way of working. From an investigative point of view analysis of the offenders MO can be used to link cases at crime scenes, however, a major stumbling block is that an offenders MO (way of working) can change. Consequently, according to criminal profilers you have to analyze behavior that transcends the MO. Innate behavior that is static and rigid; behavior that remains the same over time. This behavior relates to the things offenders are psychologically compelled to do over and above what it takes to commit the crime, and in the world of criminal profiling, this type of behavior is known as signature behavior.

Robert Keppel has written widely on criminal profiling and signature behavior and analysis. In 2002 I was fortunate enough to hear him speak at a forensic science conference in Atlanta. Entitled '*A signature analysis of the eight Whitechapel murders attributed to Jack the Ripper in 1888*' Robert Keppel's presentation sought to explain the processes involved in

24

linking murder cases through Modus Operandi and signature.

The reason I want to mention it here is that I remember thinking at the time - *and still do for that matter* – that the presentation provided an excellent way of showing how the MO and signature differ in terms of what they tell you about a particular crime. The following details are taken from Keppel's abstract in the conference proceedings.

Jack the Ripper's Modus Operandi

He attacked white female prostitutes in their 40's in a cluster of victims within a short distance of each other. The first four victims Mary Nichols, Annie Chapman, Elizabeth Stride and Catherine Eddowes were killed and found outdoors in the Whitechapel area; then he changed his MO by killing and leaving the fifth victim Mary Kelly, indoors. By choosing to murder Kelly indoors, the killer demonstrated that he was an experienced night time cat burglar and stalker, as he attacked all his victims in the early morning hours when dawn was approaching.

Jack the Ripper's Signature

Remember this relates to what he did over and above what was necessary to commit the crime, it transcends the MO.

Each victim was posed in a sexually degrading position, intentionally left that way so the discovery of the bodies would startle the people who found them. They were not concealed or hidden away, but placed in locations where they would be easily discovered. The placing of the victims on their back, grotesquely laid out with their throats cut and viscera exposed or missing, reflect the cruel reality of the killer, his total mastery over their bodies. The pleasure for the killer was demonstrating each victim's vulnerability.

Incidentally, Keppel does not believe that all the murders attributed to Jack the Ripper where in fact carried out by him. He claims that in the case of three of the Ripper's alleged victims there were fundamental differences in the signature of the crimes. However, there is no doubt that Keppel firmly believes that signature behavior represents a real and intrinsic part of an offender's personality.

"Hidden among the evidence, often gleaned from the marks and wounds on the victim's body...these signatures are the only ways the killer truly expresses himself." (Keppel & Burns).

PUTTING THEORY INTO PRACTICE

Assuming you accept the notion that criminal profiling makes it possible to elicit a behavioral signature, what do you have to do to pick up on these psychological clues? And what do you do with this information once you have it?

The best way to address these questions is to build on the information provided by John Douglas & Alan Burgess above and examine in more detail the traditional methodology employed by the FBI, whereby an investigative team works through a series of systematic stages.

Stage 1: Profiling Inputs

The first stage involves collecting as much crime related information as possible, autopsy reports, photographs of the crime scene and deceased, essentially anything that is likely to indicate what happened, how it happened and why it happened.

Stage 2: Decision Processing

Armed with the information from stage one the next step involves determining whether the crime in question can be located within a number of behavioral classifications. The FBI developed their own manual of classifications and it functions along the same lines as the system used to classify mental illness. In essence you have a checklist of signs and symptoms and if these are sufficiently present within a particular case the offender will be assigned that classification. This is why you see multi dimensional descriptions of profiled offenders e.g. organized, power assertive serial rapist.

This stage will also generate a number of more general classifications e.g. the murder type (mass, spree, serial etc); the primary motive (sexual, financial, emotional etc).

Stage 3: Crime Assessment

The principal aim of stage three is to piece together the chain of events before, during and after the commission of a crime. Essentially the profiler wants to reconstruct the crime from the perspective of both the victim and the offender.

Stage 4: The Criminal Profile

Having assessed and consolidated the information from the previous stages the profiler is now in a position to hypothesize about the type of person who committed the crime. The preliminary description will usually include details relating to the suspects sex, age, race, occupational skills, IQ, social interests, mental health status and family background.

Stage 5: Investigative Use

There are two main ways in which criminal profiling is used to assist an investigation. Firstly a detailed written report is made available to the investigating team so that they can concentrate their efforts on suspects who appear to match the profile.

The aim is to generate a reliable profile of the person who's committed the unsolved crime so that the subsequent investigative effort is much more focused. Now this may seem like an obvious point but arguably the greatest strength of profiling is that it has the potential to minimize information overload. So what exactly is meant by information overload? Well to give you two examples, in the US the search for the "green river killer" in Seattle generated 18,000 possible suspects and a single TV appeal generated 3500 tip-offs. Even more staggering was the Yorkshire Ripper inquiry in the UK which generated 268,000 named suspects and involved the police conducting 27,000 house visits.

The second way in which criminal profiling is traditionally employed within an investigation follows the arrest of a prime suspect, when the psychological aspects of the profile can be used to help develop and inform appropriate interviewing strategies.

DOES CRIMINAL PROFILING WORK?

The criminal profiling methodology developed by the FBI has been subject to sustained criticism over the years. In this section we will examine the nature of this criticism by exploring what has been said, by whom and why.

When The American Academy of Psychiatry and the Law held its annual meeting in Chicago in 2006 one of the panel discussions was entitled 'Serial Killers: From Cradle to Grave.' The panel addressed the perceived limitations of FBI profiles and among the issues raised were the following:

The notorious BTK murderer Dennis Rader who remained at large for over 30 years did not fit into the FBI's profiling methodology in relation to crime scenes.

Florida prostitute Aileen Wuornos convicted and subsequently executed for the murder of several men was effectively excluded from profiling typologies because the FBI database of convicted serial killers did not include women.

The FBI tends to categorize a crime scene as either organized or disorganized. An organized crime scene is said to highlight the control and careful planning the suspect has displayed in his/her environment when commissioning the crime; thereby pointing to an educated and socially competent individual. In contrast, a disorganized crime scene points to a lack of control and an absence of intelligent decision making. The disorganized suspect does little if anything to cover his/her tracks, pointing to a suspect who is either of low intelligence or a habitual user of drugs and/or alcohol.

On the surface this seems to be a perfectly reasonable classification system but one of the issues under discussion was the fact that crime scenes often have both organized and disorganized aspects. Dr Charles L. Scott who led the panel discussion stated that the actions of BTK murderer Dennis Rader provide a clear example of this. Scott suggests Rader's first crime scene demonstrates this ambiguity as there was clear evidence of advance planning and his domination of the environment but there were several disorganized elements as well e.g. leaving behind the Venetian blind cords he used as a strangling device. Scott also pointed to the problems associated with the fact that in developing profiles of serial killers, the FBI draws on data and findings elicited from interviews with just 36 convicted serial murderers, all of whom were male and 90% of them white; which raises the question of relevance in relation to female or non-caucasian serial killers.

According to Dr Scott *"The FBI profiling method has many positive attributes. But it also has some inherent limitations"*, and that the purpose of the panel discussion was not to critique the FBI, but acquaint forensic psychiatrists with how the FBI profiles serial killers.

In 2007 writing for the New Yorker, Malcolm Gladwell wrote a provocative article on criminal profiling entitled "Dangerous Minds." The article presents a critical review of the work of prominent FBI profilers such as John Douglas and clearly questions the usefulness of criminal profiling as an investigative methodology.

You can read Malcolm Gladwell's article in full via the following link

http://nyr.kr/DangerousMinds.

Consultant psychologist Dr Craig Jackson recently reignited the debate over the utility and effectiveness of criminal profiling arguing that criminal profiling is unscientific and potentially harmful. According to Jackson "*Behavioral profiling has never led to the direct apprehension of a serial killer or murderer, so it seems to have no real-world value.*"

As we will see in the next section, however, there is more than one approach to criminal profiling; the theoretical principles of which can differ markedly. So while it is possible to point to certain explanatory frameworks as subjective and untestable, equally, it is possible to point to more objective and testable statistical procedures being employed.

GEOGRAPHIC PROFILING

Geographical profiling is a strategic information management system employed to support serial violent crime investigation. It's formulated on the premise that the location of a crime site can provide the police with vital information. It assesses and predicts the offender's most likely place of residence, place of work, social venues and travel routes etc.

Geographic profiling consists of both quantitative (objective) scientific geographic techniques and qualitative (subjective) components e.g. a reconstruction and interpretation of the offender's mental map.

The name most closely associated with geographical profiling is Kim Rossmo who began studying geographical profiling as part of his PhD studies at Simon Fraser University (British Columbia, Canada). Rossmo studied under professors Paul and Patricia Brentingham who had developed a theoretical crime model which examined where crimes were most likely to happen, based on offender residence, workplace and leisure activity. The Brentingham model maintains that we all have an 'activity space' related to the areas in which we live, work and play and that this activity space produces a discernible pattern of movement around the city.

In relation to criminal activity, therefore, it follows that an offender has to know about a particular geographical area before he or she begins selecting crimes to commit; and where the offenders movement patterns intersect within this geographical area, will to a large extent determine where the crime takes place.

Kim Rossmo noted that the Brentingham model was examined primarily in relation to crime prevention and was interested in approaching the topic from the opposite perspective i.e. asking the question, what does the location of a crime say about where the offender might live?

Acknowledging the potential investigative use of this research the Vancouver Police Department established the world's first Geographic-Profiling Section in 1995. Since it's launch, Scotland Yard, The FBI, The New York Police Department and The Royal Canadian Mounted Police have all called upon the services of the geographic profiling section. The primary geographic technique is a computerized system known as Criminal Geographic Targeting (CGT). Put simply, spatial data i.e. data relating to time, distance and movement to and from the crime scenes is analyzed to produce a three-dimensional model known as a jeopardy surface.

The jeopardy surface contains height and color probability codes which when superimposed onto a map of the area in which the serial crimes have been committed give an indication of the likelihood of offender residence or place of work.

Although the science underpinning geographic-profiling can be difficult to comprehend, it's easy to see how this approach can offer practical assistance in the course of a criminal investigation. As Rossmo points out: "*By establishing the probability of the offender residing in various areas and displaying those results on a map, police efforts to apprehend criminals can be assisted. This information allows police departments to focus their investigative efforts, geographically prioritise suspects, and concentrate patrol efforts in those zones where the criminal predator is likely to be active".*

Geographic Profiling Process

A geographic profile would typically fit into a criminal investigation as follows:

A series of crimes is committed.

The crimes are investigated via traditional means.

Linking analysis conducted to ascertain which crimes are connected.

Psychological profile of the unknown subject conducted.

Geographical profile constructed.

New investigative strategies developed and pursued.

Geographic Profiling Methodology

In preparing a geographic profile, a number of operational procedures will be followed. These include:

Examination of the case file: Witness statements, autopsy reports & psychological profile (if available).

Inspection of the crime scene.

35

Meetings and discussions with lead investigators.
Visits to the crime sites when practical.

Analysis of local crime statistics and demographic data.

Study of street, zoning and rapid transit maps.

Overall analysis and report submission.

BECOMING A PROFILER

When you teach forensic psychology, a very common question among students is *how do I become a criminal profiler?* And thanks to the popularity of the CBS drama criminal minds, this question is now being asked more than ever. The aim of this section of the guide, therefore, is to explore whether becoming a profiler is a realistic career aspiration.

Criminal Profiling in The USA

The FBI doesn't actually have employees with the job title FBI profiler. However, as we know from our earlier discussion, special agents at the National Center for the Analysis of Violent Crime (NCAVC) at Quantico, Virginia do construct profiles of unknown offenders. They also provide case management advice, threat assessments and interviewing strategies to law enforcement agencies both home and abroad.

You cannot simply apply to the FBI and immediately become a NCAVC agent. A basic requirement is three years service as a FBI special agent. However, such is the competition for places, successful candidates tend to have up to 10 years of service behind them along with experience investigating violent and sexual crimes and abductions.

In terms of educational requirements an advanced degree in a Behavioral or Forensic Science is often listed as preferred qualification. It is possible to work at the NCAVC without being a special agent. these professional support positions include Intelligence Research Specialists, Violent Crime Resource Specialists, and Crime Analysts. These are essentially research positions so an in-depth knowledge of research methodology, data collection and analysis is required. Whether you are applying to become a NCAVC agent or a research specialist you can expect to have complete a range of written and psychometric tests.

Criminal Profiling in The UK

If you think becoming a criminal profiler in the USA seems a difficult proposition, the chances of becoming one in the UK are even more remote. In 1995 Gary Copson conducted a comprehensive survey of police use of profiling, which among other things addressed the questions, who are the profilers? What are their qualifications? What do they actually do?

Who Are The Profilers?

The Copson study found that profilers define themselves as having relevant expertise for a particular criminal investigation, although this expertise is not confined to one profession or academic discipline. In total 29 profilers were identified in the course of the study, the make-up of which was as follows: 4 forensic psychiatrists, 5 academic psychologists, 4 clinical psychologists, 6 forensic psychologists, 3 therapists (unspecified), 4 British police officers, 1 British police scientist, 1 British police data system analyst, 1 American law enforcement agency.

Qualifications?

Psychiatrists are qualified doctors of medicine who undertake postgraduate training in psychiatry.

Psychologists have both undergraduate and postgraduate degrees in their specialist area and may have secured chartered status through the governing body that oversees their professional development.

Police officers who undertake profiling work have usually studied psychology as a postgraduate.

What Do They Do?

As with any form of profiling, the principal aim is to generate a behavioral composite of an unknown offender so that it tells you something about the personality of the individual.

In the Copson study 184 accounts of profiling are documented. In 111 of these cases the profiler put his/her advice into writing. An analysis of the content of these written reports revealed 10 main areas of advice.

1. Features of the offence

2. Character of the offence

3. Origins of the offender

4. Present circumstances of the offender

5. Criminality of the offender

6. Geography of the offender

7. Predicted future behavior of the offender

8. Interview strategies to be adopted

9. Threat assessment

10. Specific police recommendations

Still Want To Be A Profiler?

Good for you, but please bear in mind that very few people get to do it as a form of career. My advice would be to concentrate on doing well within a broader field e.g. psychology. While you're doing so, there is no reason why you can't continue pursuing your interest in profiling, for instance by doing a criminal profiling related thesis or dissertation.

I thought it would be appropriate to conclude this section by documenting the definitive answer given by the FBI to the question How Do I Become a FBI Profiler?

I Just Want To Be An FBI Profiler Where Do I Begin The Application Process?

You first need to realize the FBI does not have a job called FBI Profiler. The tasks commonly associated with a FBI profiler are performed by Supervisory Special Agents assigned to the National Center for the Analysis of Violent Crime (NCAVC) at Quantico, Virginia.

These FBI Special Agents don't get vibes or experience psychic flashes while walking around fresh crime scenes. It is an exciting world of investigation and research—a world of inductive and deductive reasoning; crime-solving experience;

and knowledge of criminal behavior, facts, and statistical probabilities.

In addition to constructing "profiles" (descriptions of the traits and characteristics of unknown offenders in specific cases), the NCAVC staff provides many services to law enforcement agencies around the world. These services include major case management advice; threat assessment; and strategies for investigation, interviewing, or prosecution.

What Is An average Day Like For A NCAVC Special Agent?

One of the attractions of the position, and indeed most FBI jobs, is that there is no "average" day. Many days might be spent in a normal office setting, working about 10 hours per day. The Special Agents might review crime scene photos and case materials to prepare an analysis for the requesting agency. Perhaps investigators or prosecutors meet with a group of Special Agents to discuss their cases.

On any given day, emergency calls from FBI offices, local police, prosecutors, etc., interrupt a Special Agent's plans. When an emergency call comes in, a group of Special Agents familiar with the type of case involved might gather for a telephone conference with the requesting agency.
NCAVC Special Agents and Professional Support staff also share results of research and general information about the unit and services through presentations to such audiences as professional conferences or law enforcement training programs. Staff members publish articles in professional journals regarding research and practices of the NCAVC.

What Basic Requirements Do I Need To Join The NCAVC?

You do not complete training (at Quantico, Virginia), and instantly get assigned to the NCAVC. One of the basic requirements is that you must have served as an FBI Special Agent for 3 years, but because the positions are so competitive, individuals selected usually possess 8 to 10 years of experience as a Special Agent.

The NCAVC employs Special Agents with a variety of backgrounds; however, the most important qualifications include overall experience as an investigator specializing in violent crimes, particularly homicides, rapes, child abductions, and threats.

What Type of Degree Is Preferred For NCAVC Special Agent Positions?

The jobs within the NCAVC typically require experience and demonstrated abilities as a Special Agent rather than specific degree majors. There are usually no set degree criteria, although job advertisements typically list an advanced degree in a Behavioral or Forensic Science as a "preferred qualification."

Applicants interested in eventual employment with the FBI's NCAVC should pursue a degree in the discipline that most interests them. Remember, becoming a Special Agent does not guarantee eventual assignment to the NCAVC.

What Type of Training Is Available Or Required For NCAVC Staff Once They Are Selected?

Staff members are strongly encouraged to take classes and attend training that will enhance their work products. Periodically, a structured training program of more than 500 hours is run for newly assigned personnel. Special Agents and Professional Support staff join professional associations and actively participate in annual conferences. Through a monthly "staff development program," prominent speakers are brought in for a day of discussion on topics of interest.

I Do Not Want To Be A Special Agent, But I Do Want To Work In The Unit. What Professional Support Positions Are Available?

One of the missions of the NCAVC is to conduct research into violent crime from a law enforcement perspective. Of primary interest to researchers is how the offenders in the study committed their crimes and how they avoided detection, identification, apprehension, and conviction. Professional Support staff are integral members of the research teams within the NCAVC. These positions include Intelligence Research Specialists, Violent Crime Resource Specialists, and Crime Analysts.

Qualifications for the Professional Support positions will vary with the specific job, but most require a solid foundation in research and analysis. The NCAVC also hires Major Case Specialists. These GS-14 jobs require a background in investigations and are generally held by retired police officers with experience in interpersonal crimes, particularly homicide.

Competitive candidates will be required to complete a battery of written tests and, in some cases, specialized testing in their field of expertise. If you pass these tests, you may be eligible for an interview based upon your overall qualifications, your competitiveness with other candidates, and the needs of the FBI. Successful completion of the written test and an interview will be followed by a thorough background investigation that will include: credit and arrest checks; interviews of associates; contacts with personal and business references, past employers and neighbors; and verification of educational achievements.

Certain factors will disqualify a candidate from selection as a Special Agent. These factors include: conviction of a felony or major misdemeanor; use of illegal drugs; or failure to pass a drug-screening test. All candidates will be given a polygraph examination to determine the veracity of information provided in their application for employment, to include the extent of any illegal drug usage and issues surrounding security concerns.

A medical examination must be passed to determine physical suitability for the Special Agent position. You are expected to be physically fit to participate in the demanding physical training conducted at the FBI Academy, and upon graduation, to execute the duties of a law enforcement officer. All candidates must meet a standardized weight to height ratio and/or body fat requirement to be qualified for appointment.

ACCESS FBI PROFILING PUBLICATIONS

The FBI vault is an electronic reading room which contains documents and other media which have been scanned from paper into digital copies so that they can be read in the comfort of your home.

Among the 6,700 documents is an amazing criminal profiling collection which includes full access to all the seminal criminal profiling publications written by members of the Behavioral Sciences Units, National Center for The Analysis of Violent Crime, at the FBI Academy, Quantico, Virginia. It is difficult to underestimate the importance of this body of work in the history and development of criminal profiling

You can access the FBI Vault criminal profiling collection via the following link.

http://vault.fbi.gov/Criminal%20Profiling

A FINAL WORD

I sincerely hope that you now have a greater understanding of both the mechanics of criminal profiling and the questions it raises when employed as an investigative tool.

Criminal Profiling is as fascinating as it is controversial and its usefulness within a criminal investigation will continue to be the subject of considerable debate. With this in mind, I also sincerely hope that your interest in criminal profiling will continue and that you will engage with the debate surrounding it as it moves forward.

The aim of argument, or of discussion, should not be victory, but progress (Joseph Joubert).

Psychology Student Guide

Finally, if you are a psychology student, or you are thinking about becoming one, you might find my Psychology Student Guide useful. Drawing on my experience as both a student and then a University lecturer in Psychology, this guide is designed to inform students at every stage of their educational journey. See following link for full details.

www.amazon.com/dp/B009ZC2UOS

Wishing you all the very best

David Webb BSc (hons), MSc

www.all-about-psychology.com

9397950R00027

Printed in Great Britain
by Amazon.co.uk, Ltd.,
Marston Gate.